Life To Me, Life To You

By Emily Godwin

Co-Pilot Publishing LLC, Blountsville, AL 35031
Printed on acid-free paper

LOC 2024941693
ISBN: 979-8-3302-7799-5

Co-Pilot Publishing, 2024

About the Author

Emily Godwin is an elementary school teacher, going on four years. She graduated from the University of Georgia with a Bachelor's degree in elementary education. She decided to further her education with a Master's degree in education and a Specialist's in Instructional Technology. With plans to pursue her Doctorate degree, mental training and learning is her passion. She has a lust for life itself and finding the meaning behind it. With many years pondering, she's found that life when you're young is to be enjoyed, alongside hard work and dedication. This book is meant to help children understand why they are here and that life can be found all around, if one only opens their eyes.

Dedication

To my parents, David and Andrea, for showing me the meaning of life itself and how it should be lived with joy, love, and hard work.

DO YOU WONDER
WHY YOU'RE HERE?

WHICH DIRECTION
YOU SHOULD STEER?

WHERE MIGHT YOU GO?
WHO MIGHT YOU MEET?

I'M HERE TO TELL YOU
WHY LIFE IS SO SWEET.

LIFE CAN GET TOUGH,
BUT NO NEED TO GRUFF.

DO YOUR BEST
TO BE YOUR BEST,
LIFE WILL TAKE CARE
OF THE REST.

LIFE IS BIG SMILES AND
"STAY-FOR-A-WHILE'S".
IT'S FAMILY TIME,
THE DOORBELL CHIME

LIFE TO ME IS SOMETHING FREE.

IT'S SOMETHING
BEAUTIFUL,
FUN,
AND HAPPY.

A DOG'S BARK,
PLAYING WITH FRIENDS AT THE PARK.

A SWING-SET, A SLIDE,
THE OCEAN AND ITS' TIDE...

THIS IS WHAT LIFE IS ALL ABOUT.

LIFE IS CHILDREN PLAYING TAG,
RUNNING IN A ZIG-ZAG...

HAVING FUN OUTSIDE,
IN THE SUN

LIFE IS FULL OF LAUGHS, IT'S A ROAD
WITH MANY DIFFERENT PATHS.

IT'S THE MOON AT NIGHT, THE WAY IT
SHINES SO BRIGHT.

IT'S THE SUNRISE IN THE MORNING AND
EVEN THE RAIN...
WHEN IT'S POURING.

YOU SEE,
IN ALL THINGS AROUND,
LIFE CAN BE FOUND...

SLEEPING SAFE AND SOUND
OR THE NOISINESS OF A
CONSTRUCTION WORKERS POUND.

Aa B
1 2 3

LIFE IS
ANIMALS AND PEOPLE.

A FIREMAN, A DOCTOR,
A TEACHER...

AN UNDISCOVERED CREATURE.

LIFE IS FULL OF FUN AND FIRST TIMES,

BIG TREES TO CLIMB AND WORDS THAT RHYME.

HAPPY IS EVERYWHERE
YOU ARE.

IT'S SINGING, JUMPING,
OR PLAYING IN THE YARD.

LIFE CAN BE GIVING A HUG
TO SOMEONE YOU LOVE,

OR WATCHING THE STARS
UP ABOVE.

LIFE TO ME IS EVERYTHING.
IT'S ABOUT LEARNING WHAT'S NEW.

WHAT WILL LIFE BE TO
YOU?

9 798330 277995